SUPER CUTE!

Baby
Zebras

by Megan Borgert-Spaniol

BELLWETHER MEDIA • MINNEAPOLIS, MN

Note to Librarians, Teachers, and Parents:

Blastoff! Readers are carefully developed by literacy experts and combine standards-based content with developmentally appropriate text.

Level 1 provides the most support through repetition of high-frequency words, light text, predictable sentence patterns, and strong visual support.

Level 2 offers early readers a bit more challenge through varied simple sentences, increased text load, and less repetition of high-frequency words.

Level 3 advances early-fluent readers toward fluency through increased text and concept load, less reliance on visuals, longer sentences, and more literary language.

Level 4 builds reading stamina by providing more text per page, increased use of punctuation, greater variation in sentence patterns, and increasingly challenging vocabulary.

Level 5 encourages children to move from "learning to read" to "reading to learn" by providing even more text, varied writing styles, and less familiar topics.

Whichever book is right for your reader, Blastoff! Readers are the perfect books to build confidence and encourage a love of reading that will last a lifetime!

This edition first published in 2017 by Bellwether Media, Inc.

No part of this publication may be reproduced in whole or in part without written permission of the publisher. For information regarding permission, write to Bellwether Media, Inc., Attention: Permissions Department, 5357 Penn Avenue South, Minneapolis, MN 55419.

Library of Congress Cataloging-in-Publication Data

Names: Borgert-Spaniol, Megan, 1989- , author.
Title: Baby Zebras / by Megan Borgert-Spaniol.
Description: Minneapolis, MN : Bellwether Media, Inc., 2017. | Series:
   Blastoff! Readers. Super Cute! | Includes bibliographical references and
   index. | Audience: Ages 5 to 8. | Audience: Grades K to 3.
Identifiers: LCCN 2016032030 (print) | LCCN 2016038138 (ebook) | ISBN
   9781626175488 (hardcover : alk. paper) | ISBN 9781681032771 (ebook)
Subjects: LCSH: Zebras–Infancy–Juvenile literature.
Classification: LCC QL737.U62 B67 2017 (print) | LCC QL737.U62 (ebook) | DDC
   599.665/71392–dc23
LC record available at https://lccn.loc.gov/2016032030

Editor: Betsy Rathburn   Designer: Brittany McIntosh

Printed in the United States of America, North Mankato, MN.

Table of Contents

Zebra Foal!

A baby zebra is called a foal. A **newborn** foal has brown stripes.

The foal has long legs. They **wobble** as it tries to stand.

The foal can run an hour after birth.

Time With Mom

Mom and her foal stay close together. This helps them **bond**.

Mom **grooms** her foal. She licks its hair clean.

The foal drinks mom's milk when hungry.

Joining the Herd

Soon they join the **herd**. The foal can find mom by her stripes, smell, and sound.

The foal is safer
in the herd.
Its stripes help
it blend in.

The herd runs
fast when
predators are
near. This foal
can keep up!

Glossary

bond—to become close

grooms—cleans

herd—a group of zebras that travels together

newborn—just recently born

predators—animals that hunt other animals for food

wobble—to move in a shaky way

To Learn More

AT THE LIBRARY

Owings, Lisa. *Meet a Baby Zebra.*
Minneapolis, Minn.: Lerner Publishing Group,
2016.

Riggs, Kate. *Zebras.* Mankato, Minn.: Creative
Education, 2015.

Zobel, Derek. *Zebras.* Minneapolis, Minn.:
Bellwether Media, 2011.

ON THE WEB

Learning more about zebras
is as easy as 1, 2, 3.

1. Go to www.factsurfer.com.

2. Enter "zebras" into the search box.

3. Click the "Surf" button and you will see a
   list of related web sites.

With factsurfer.com, finding more information
is just a click away.

Index

The images in this book are reproduced through the courtesy of: Justin Black, front cover; Franzisca Guedel, pp. 4-5; Newspix/ Zuma Press, pp. 6-7; NaturePL/ SuperStock, pp. 8-9; Leigh Gregg, pp. 10-11; Gerard Lacz Images/ SuperStock, pp. 12-13; James Hager/ Glow Images, pp. 14-15; ksumano, pp. 16-17; Katja Forster, pp. 18-19; blickwinkel/ Alamy, pp. 20-21.